Presented to

_____

Given by

_____

Published by Barbour Publishing, Inc., P.O. Box 719, Uhrichsville, Ohio 44683
www.barbourbooks.com

 Member of the
Evangelical Christian
Publishers Association

Printed in China.

TWELVE SACRED SONGS
IN WORD AND MUSIC

HYMNS OF

God's love

DANIEL PARTNER

BARBOUR
PUBLISHING, INC.

This is real love.

It is not that we loved God,
but that he loved us
and sent his Son
as a sacrifice
to take away our sins.
1 John 4:10

THE Bible tells all about Jesus Christ, a man unlike anyone who ever lived. He was the Son of God, the expression of God's love. This little book tells about this love in the lyrics of twelve hymns. One of these, written by Charles Wesley, begins like this,

Love divine, all loves excelling,
joy of heaven to earth come down. . .

That's just another way of saying, "For God so loved the world that he gave his only Son" (John 3:16).

In addition to the lyrics, the meaning of each hymn and stories of the hymns' writers are told in short, devotional-style articles. You'll also find the music to these hymns in the companion compact disc included in this package. All this is presented to you with the prayer that you may "know the love of Christ that surpasses knowledge, so that you may be filled with all the fullness of God" (Ephesians 3:19 NRSV).

Daniel Partner
Sisters, Oregon

O the Deep, Deep Love of Jesus

Words: Samuel Trevor Francis

Music: Thomas J. Williams

O the deep, deep love of Je - sus, Vast, un - meas - ured,

bound - less, free! Roll - ing as a might - y o - cean

In its full - ness o - ver me, Un - der - neath me,

all a - round me, Is the cur - rent of Thy love; Lead - ing on-ward,

lead - ing home - ward To my glo - rious rest a - bove.

O THE DEEP, DEEP LOVE OF JESUS

O the deep, deep love of Jesus, vast, unmeasured, boundless, free!
Rolling as a mighty ocean in its fullness over me!
Underneath me, all around me, is the current of Thy love
Leading onward, leading homeward to Thy glorious rest above!

O the deep, deep love of Jesus, spread His praise from
    shore to shore!
How he loveth, ever loveth, changeth never, nevermore!
How he watches o'er His loved ones, died to call them all
    His own;
How for them intercedeth, watcheth o'er them from the throne!

O the deep, deep love of Jesus, love of every love the best!
'Tis an ocean full of blessing, 'tis a haven giving rest!
O the deep, deep love of Jesus, 'tis a heaven of heavens to me;
And it lifts me up to glory, for it lifts me up to Thee!

SOME people say that Jesus Christ is only one of many prophets of God. Each of these, they say, added something to our understanding of God and the right way to live our lives. But the Bible, which tells about Christ, does not say that. Far from being like anyone else who ever lived, Jesus was the Son of God. And because God is love, love marks Christ as entirely unique.

But what is love? One chapter of the Bible describes it thoroughly and in doing so paints a portrait for us of Jesus Christ; here are its first three verses:

If I could speak in any language in heaven or on earth but didn't love others, I would only be making meaningless noise like a loud gong or a clanging cymbal. If I had the gift of prophecy, and if I knew all the mysteries of the future and knew everything about everything, but didn't love others, what good would I be? And if I had the gift of faith so that I could speak to a mountain and make it move, without love I would be no good to anybody. If I gave everything I have to the poor and even sacrificed my body, I could boast about it; but if I didn't love others, I would be of no value whatsoever (1 Corinthians 13:1-3).

These verses describe the other prophets and holy men of history. They each were able to do some or all of the six amazing things listed here. Without love, however, these abilities are worthless for God's purpose.

But what is love?

The next five verses of 1 Corinthians 13 provide an answer:

Love is patient and kind. Love is not jealous or boastful or proud or rude. Love does not demand its own way. Love is not irritable, and it keeps no record of when it has been wronged. It is never glad about injustice but rejoices whenever the truth wins out. Love never gives up, never loses faith, is always hopeful, and endures through every circumstance. Love will last forever, but prophecy and speaking in unknown languages and special knowledge will all disappear (vv. 4–8).

Do you embody all these qualities? Does anyone? No. These verses do not describe loving traits that belonged to Jesus Christ or anyone else. Rather they are describing Jesus Christ himself. He *is* love.

Next, in 1 Corinthians 13:9–12, the author describes himself and everyone else—we know only a little about love, we see spiritual things imperfectly, and our knowledge of divine things is at best "partial and incomplete." But the day will come when we will know everything completely, just like God knows us now.

Then comes the last verse in the chapter—the last word on love. "There are three things that will endure—faith, hope, and love—and the greatest of these is love" (v. 13). The greatest is *love*.

Lord, I thank you for your love.

Grant that I will love others as you do—

freely, completely, selflessly.

And in loving others,

may I spread your praise from shore to shore!

Dear friends,
let us continue to love one another,
for love comes from God.

Anyone who loves is born of God
and knows God.

But anyone who does not love
does not know God—

for God is love.
1 John 4:7–8

Amazing Grace

Words: John Newton   Music: Traditional American Melody

A - maz - ing grace! how sweet the sound—

That saved a wretch like me!

I once was lost but now am found,

Was blind but now I see.

AMAZING GRACE

Amazing grace! How sweet the sound
That saved a wretch like me!
I once was lost, but now am found;
Was blind, but now I see.

'Twas grace that taught my heart to fear,
And grace my fears relieved;
How precious did that grace appear
The hour I first believed.

Through many dangers, toils and snares,
I have already come;
'Tis grace hath brought me safe thus far,
And grace will lead me home.

The Lord has promised good to me,
His Word my hope secures;
He will my Shield and Portion be,
As long as life endures.

Yea, when this flesh and heart shall fail,
And mortal life shall cease,
I shall possess, within the veil,
A life of joy and peace.

The earth shall soon dissolve like snow,
The sun forbear to shine;
But God, Who called me here below,
Shall be forever mine.

When we've been there ten thousand years,
Bright shining as the sun,
We've no less days to sing God's praise
Than when we'd first begun.

> *"I know this:*
> # *I was blind,*
> ### *and now I can see!"*
> John 9:25

I WAS raised in a good, churchgoing family, yet I never heard the hymn "Amazing Grace" sung in church. I find this amazing in itself, since it is possibly the most-played hymn in America. I first heard it sung by the pop singer Judy Collins–which for me is ironic, since Judy Collins and I attended the same church when I was a child. I don't remember, but I'm told she played the piano there. Maybe she played "Amazing Grace"–I can't say. Anyway, I left the church and went on my way and finally heard the beautiful words of this song somewhere far out in the world.

Eventually grace appeared to me in the hour I first believed, just as it did to John Newton, the author of this and many other hymns. Newton was also the author of the epitaph for his own gravestone.

Here's what it says:

> *JOHN NEWTON, Clerk*
> *Once an infidel and libertine*
> *A servant of slaves in Africa,*
> *Was, by the rich mercy of our Lord and Savior*
> *JESUS CHRIST,*
> *restored, pardoned, and appointed to preach*
> *the Gospel which he had long labored to destroy.*
> *He ministered,*
> *Near sixteen years in Olney, in Bucks,*
> *And twenty-eight years in this Church.*

Newton was born in 1725 in London, England. After two years of schooling he went to sea with his father. He was eleven years old. His life seems to have been as amazing as his hymn—that of a reckless, debauched seaman. He was once flogged as a deserter and was himself deserted on the shores of Africa. There, he was enslaved for fifteen months. In 1748, Newton was piloting a waterlogged ship on a storm-plagued voyage from Africa to England. He thought his end was near. That was when grace began to teach his heart to fear.

He remained at sea and became captain of a ship working in the slave trade. But Newton returned to England to stay in 1854. He worked as a clerk in the surveyor's office of the Port of Liverpool. Newton studied Hebrew and Greek, became acquainted with the religious leaders John Whitefield and John Wesley, and was eventually ordained in the Church of England. He became curate at Olney, Bucks, in 1764. There he formed a lifelong friendship with William Cowper, author of "God Moves in a Mysterious Way" and many other hymns. The two wrote and published the *Olney Hymns,* which included "Amazing Grace." John Newton's autobiography, *An Authentic Narrative,* was published in 1764.

How is it possible for a man to be drawn out of such a life and become such a gift to the church and the world? His mother had died when he was a child; so who prayed for John Newton? Apparently, someone did.

I know that grace appeared to me because of the prayers of my mother and others in the Women's Society of Christian Service at the Wheat Ridge Methodist Church. My experience of amazing grace compels me to persist in prayer for my own children.

Lord, I know that someday my flesh and heart will fail, my mortal life shall cease. But I thank you that I possess your invisible life of joy and peace. The earth will soon dissolve like snow, and the sun refuse to shine.

But I worship you because
I know you are forever mine.

Come and listen,
all you who fear God,

and I will tell you
what he did for me.
Psalm 66:16

Love Divine, All Loves Excelling

Words: Charles Wesley

Music: John Zundel

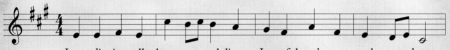

Love di-vine, all loves ex - cel-ling, Joy of heav'n, to earth come down;

Fix in us Thy hum-ble dwell-ing, All Thy faith-ful mer-cies crown.

Je - sus, Thou art all com - pas-sion, Pure, un-bound-ed love Thou art;

Vis - it us with Thy sal - va-tion, En - ter ev - 'ry trem - bling heart.

LOVE DIVINE,
ALL LOVES EXCELLING

Love divine, all loves excelling,
Joy of heaven to earth come down;
Fix in us Thy humble dwelling;
All Thy faithful mercies crown!
Jesus, Thou art all compassion,
Pure unbounded love Thou art;
Visit us with Thy salvation;
Enter every trembling heart.

Breathe, O breathe Thy loving Spirit,
Into every troubled breast!
Let us all in Thee inherit;
Let us find that second rest.
Take away our bent to sinning;
Alpha and Omega be;
End of faith, as its Beginning,
Set our hearts at liberty.

> *We know how much God loves us,*
> *and we have put our trust in him. God is love,*
> *and all who live in love live in God,*
> ## *and God lives in them.*
> 1 John 4:16

THE author of this hymn, Charles Wesley, and his brother John were sons of Samuel Wesley, a Church of England cleric, and his devout and capable wife Susanna. They attended Oxford University, followed their father's footsteps into the ministry, and became the founders of the Methodist Church.

While at Oxford, Charles Wesley studied classical literature. As it turned out, he became a significant figure in English literature— "Love Divine, All Loves Excelling" is one of the more than three thousand hymns written by Wesley. John Dryden (1631–1700) is among Wesley's fellow poets. In fact, Wesley probably copied the pattern of rhyme and meter in "Love Divine, All Loves Excelling" from Dryden's poem about Camelot titled "King Arthur." The similarity is clearly seen: "Fairest Isle, all isles excelling, seats of pleasure and of love," wrote Dryden. "Love divine, all loves excelling, joy of heaven to earth come down," sang Wesley.

While Dryden wrote of King Arthur's legendary kingdom, Wesley focused on Jesus Christ's heavenly kingdom. Arthur's is fantasy; Christ's is reality. From the first line of his hymn, Wesley outlines some features of the heavenly kingdom that are probably recognizable to people who believe.

The coming of the kingdom began with the incarnation of Jesus Christ—the birth of God in humanity: "Love divine, all loves excelling, joy of heaven to earth come down." The kingdom is established as Christ makes his home in the hearts of believers: "Fix in us Thy humble dwelling; All Thy faithful mercies crown!" Since God has begun the work of settling the kingdom on earth, Wesley prays that Christ would finish the work: "Alpha and Omega be; end of faith, as its beginning, set

Come, Almighty to deliver, Let us all Thy life receive.

our hearts at liberty."

Next comes a prayer for Christ's return—for the physical manifestation of the Kingdom of God. "Suddenly return and never, never more Thy temples leave" is the poet's eloquent plea before he describes a view of the kingdom's bliss:

Thee we would be always blessing,
Serve Thee as Thy hosts above,
Pray and praise Thee without ceasing,
Glory in Thy perfect love.

As a minister in the Church of England, Charles Wesley led worshipers in the Lord's Prayer. Many Christians frequently repeat the familiar words of Matthew 6:9–13. With his hymn "Love Divine, All Loves Excelling," Wesley had found a fresh way to utter the hope of all the ages—"Your kingdom come. Your will be done, on earth as it is in heaven" (v. 10 NRSV). "Finish, then, Thy new creation," the hymn writer says. "Pure and spotless let us be. Let us see Thy great salvation perfectly restored in Thee. Changed from glory into glory, till in heaven we take our place, till we cast our crowns before Thee, lost in wonder, love, and praise."

Jesus, Lord, I pray for that moment when the last trumpet sounds, when the dead are raised imperishable and my mortal body puts on immortality, when death is swallowed up in your victory, and the Kingdom of God is seen on this earth.

Then I saw a new heaven and a new earth,
for the old heaven and the old earth had disappeared.
And the sea was also gone.

And I saw the holy city, the new Jerusalem,
coming down from God out of heaven

like a beautiful bride
prepared for her husband.
Revelation 21:1–2

27

Jesus, Lover of My Soul

Words: Charles Wesley

Music: John B. Dykes

Je - sus, Lov - er of my soul, Let me to Thy bo - som fly,

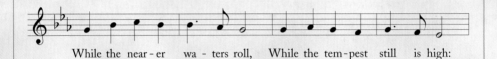

While the near - er wa - ters roll, While the tem - pest still is high:

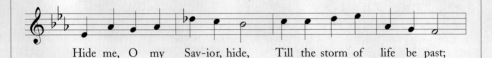

Hide me, O my Sav - ior, hide, Till the storm of life be past;

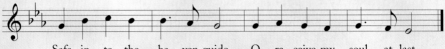

Safe in - to the ha - ven guide, O re - ceive my soul at last.

JESUS, LOVER OF MY SOUL

Jesus, lover of my soul, let me to Thy bosom fly,
While the nearer waters roll, while the tempest still is high.
Hide me, O my Savior, hide, till the storm of life is past;
Safe into the haven guide; O receive my soul at last.

Other refuge have I none, hangs my helpless soul on Thee;
Leave, ah! leave me not alone, still support and comfort me.
All my trust on Thee is stayed, all my help from Thee I bring;
Cover my defenseless head with the shadow of Thy wing.

Wilt Thou not regard my call? Wilt Thou not accept my prayer?
Lo! I sink, I faint, I fall–Lo! on Thee I cast my care;
Reach me out Thy gracious hand! While I of
      Thy strength receive,
Hoping against hope I stand, dying, and behold, I live.

Guard me
as the apple of your eye.
Hide me
in the shadow of your wings.

Protect me
from wicked people who attack me,
from murderous enemies who surround me.

Psalm 17:8–9

THIS hymn is one of the more than six thousand completed hymns of Charles Wesley (1707–1788). In addition, at his death Wesley left about three thousand in manuscript form. George Frideric Handel, composer of the *Messiah,* wrote music specifically for some of these hymns. Among Wesley's best-known hymns are "Love Divine, All Loves Excelling," "Hark, the Herald Angels Sing," "Christ the Lord Is Ris'n Today," "Soldiers of Christ, Arise," and "Rejoice, the Lord Is King."

Charles Wesley was the English clergyman, poet, and hymn writer who started the Methodist movement in the Church of England along with his elder brother John. He was an eloquent preacher and translated the gospel message into hymns that were important means of evangelism. But Charles and John Wesley were eventually estranged from each other when Charles interfered with his brother's proposed marriage. He soon withdrew from active leadership of the Methodist societies. Charles was more deeply attached to the Church of England than was John, and did not approve of his brother's decision to independently ordain preachers. However, none of these things happened before Charles had made an indelible mark upon the church through his work as an evangelist and hymn writer.

Here is an interesting story of how Wesley came to write, "Jesus, Lover of My Soul." It is impossible to tell if this story is true but it does make for a good illustration of the meaning of the hymn. The narrative is from the family tradition of the Hoover family of Bellefonte, Pennsylvania.

Charles Wesley was preaching in the fields of the parish of Killyleagh, County Down, Ireland, when he was attacked by men who did not approve of his doctrines. *Jesus, lover of my soul, let me to*

Thou, O Christ, art all I want, more than all in Thee I find.

Thy bosom fly! And indeed Wesley did. He sought refuge in a house on the nearby Island Barn Farm. *Hide me, O my Savior, hide.* The woman of the farm, Jane Lowrie Moore, told him to hurry to the garden and hide there in the milk house. *Till the storm of life is past; safe into the haven guide.* Soon the mob came and demanded the fugitive. She tried to quiet them by offering them some refreshing milk.

Other refuge have I none, hangs my helpless soul on Thee. She hurried to the milkhouse and directed Mr. Wesley to get through the rear window and hide under the hedge near a little brook. *Let the healing streams abound; make and keep me pure within.* In that hiding place, Wesley wrote his hymn. *Thou of life the fountain art, freely let me take of Thee.*

Dearest God, lead me to the towering rock of safety, for you are my safe refuge, a fortress where my enemies cannot reach me.

Let me live forever in your sanctuary, safe beneath the shelter of your wings!

(see Psalm 61:1–4)

I love you, LORD;
you are my strength.

The LORD *is my rock, my fortress, and my savior;
my God is my rock, in whom I find protection.*

*He is my shield,
the strength of my salvation,
and my stronghold.*

I will call on the LORD,
*who is worthy of praise,
for he saves me from my enemies.*

Psalm 18:1–3

Jesus, Thy Blood and Righteousness

Words: Ludwig von Zinzendorf
Translated by John Wesley

Music: William Gardner's Sacred Melodies

Je - sus, Thy blood and right - eous - ness

My beau - ty are, my glo - rious dress;

'Midst flam - ing worlds, in these ar - rayed, With

joy shall I lift up my head.

JESUS, THY BLOOD AND RIGHTEOUSNESS

Jesus, Thy blood and righteousness
My beauty are, my glorious dress;
'Midst flaming worlds, in these arrayed,
With joy shall I lift up my head.

Bold shall I stand in Thy great day;
For who aught to my charge shall lay?
Fully absolved through these I am
From sin and fear, from guilt and shame.

When from the dust of death I rise
To claim my mansion in the skies,
Ev'n then this shall be all my plea,
Jesus hath lived, hath died, for me.

As many of you as were baptized into Christ
have clothed yourselves with Christ.
Galatians 3:27 NRSV

HERE is a word most people don't like to hear—*sin*. Sin is such a loathsome thing that it is often banned from conversation, polite or otherwise.

Sin is the word the Bible uses in reference to the separation of humanity from God and the effects of this separation. Sin is the problem that God had to solve if his divine plan was to proceed.

The trouble began in a garden where a snake said to a woman, "Did God really say you must not eat any of the fruit in the garden?" (Genesis 3:1). God hadn't really said that; maybe Eve was flustered by the question. Anyway, she and her husband tasted the fruit of the one tree they were forbidden to harvest. Their disobedience allowed sin to enter and the fall from God began. Immediately the couple covered their sudden nakedness with clothes made of leaves (v. 7). The story goes on to describe some disagreeable results of the fall—

the pains of childbearing, endless toil with little result, and death (3:14–19).

Picture this primal episode of the human drama: The man and woman, representatives of our whole race, are standing together talking with God wearing wilting leaves–their pathetic solution to sin. Unless something is done, their sin will be forever apparent to the eyes of God. So God stepped in and made clothing from animal skins for Adam and his wife (Genesis 3:21).

Nicolaus Ludwig von Zinzendorf, the author of this hymn, knew that the reality of this clothing is Jesus Christ. His words in the hymn's first verse are not merely poetic, they are truth:

Jesus, Thy blood and righteousness
My beauty are, my glorious dress;
'Midst flaming worlds, in these arrayed,
With joy shall I lift up my head.

God made clothes for the first couple–and he still makes "clothes" today. Needless to say, Christ is many things to a believer. But the following item is at the top of the list: God has placed the believers in Christ. We wear him like clothing. In Christ, we become the righteousness of God (2 Corinthians 5:21 NRSV). This is God's solution to the problem of sin. "So," says the apostle Paul, "if anyone is *in Christ,* there is a new creation: everything old has passed away; see, everything has become new!" (v. 17 NRSV, author's emphasis).

The fall from God brought death into humanity. It caused us to be outcasts from the paradise of God. But in Christ we are restored. So sing along with Count Zinzendorf with rejoicing:

O let the dead now hear Thy voice;
Now bid Thy banished ones rejoice;
Their beauty this, their glorious dress,
Jesus, Thy blood and righteousness.

Dear God, thank you that I am in Christ where I don't have to fabricate my own righteousness. I am so grateful that here I have your righteousness, the righteousness that is based on faith in Christ.

And now, all glory to God,
who is able to keep you from stumbling,

and who will bring you
into his glorious presence
innocent of sin and with great joy.
Jude 1:24

41

In Heavenly Love Abiding

Words: Anna L. Waring

Music: D. Jenkins

In heav'n-ly love a-bid-ing, No change my heart shall fear, And safe is such con-fid-ing, For noth-ing chan-ges here. The storm may roar with-out me, My heart may low be laid; But God is round a-bout me, And can I be dis-mayed?

In Heavenly Love Abiding

In heavenly love abiding, no change my heart shall fear.
And safe in such confiding, for nothing changes here.
The storm may roar without me, my heart may low be laid,
But God is round about me, and can I be dismayed?

Wherever He may guide me, no want shall turn me back.
My Shepherd is beside me, and nothing can I lack.
His wisdom ever waking, His sight is never dim.
He knows the way He's taking, and I will walk with Him.

Green pastures are before me, which yet I have not seen.
Bright skies will soon be over me, where darkest clouds
    have been.
My hope I cannot measure, my path to life is free.
My Savior has my treasure, and He will walk with me.

God is our refuge and strength,
  always ready to help in times of trouble.
  ## So we will not fear,
  even if earthquakes come
  and the mountains crumble into the sea.
  Let the oceans roar and foam.
  Let the mountains tremble as the waters surge!

A river brings joy to the city of our God,
  the sacred home of the Most High.

Psalm 46:1–4

I'VE been reading the Bible steadily for many years. Maybe you read it too. If so, you know that the New Testament tells the good news about Jesus Christ. Yes, it tells about a lot of other things, but it especially tells of Jesus and the effect that his life, death, and resurrection had upon the earth.

When I think about this, and about Anna Waring's hymn, two

verses from the New Testament come to mind. One is Hebrews 13:8–"Jesus Christ is the same yesterday, today, and forever." The other is James 1:17–"Whatever is good and perfect comes to us from God above, who created all heaven's lights. Unlike them, he never changes or casts shifting shadows." These verses show that God does not change. But think back over your reading of the New Testament. Isn't it about change–the change brought about by the birth of Christ? Naturally, when a child is born, many changes for its family came along, too. God is the Father of all (see Ephesians 3:14–15) so the birth of the Son of God was going to bring about enormous changes for all creation.

For example, when the old prophet Simeon blessed the infant Jesus in the Temple, he said to Mary, "This child will be rejected by many in Israel, and it will be their undoing. But he will be the greatest joy to many others" (Luke 2:34)–a hint of the big changes that were to come. And how Jesus changed things!–first individual lives and eventually entire societies and cultures. This change was seen not long after his resurrection when the apostles were spreading the gospel through Asia Minor and Greece. They came to Thessalonica where many people believed their message about the Messiah. But a mob formed to oppose them and set the city in an uproar. The mob cried out to the magistrates, "Paul and Silas have turned the rest of the world upside down, and now they are here disturbing *our* city!" (Acts 17:6, author's emphasis). To this day there is no more profound change for a person than to confess sincere faith in Christ.

This little hymn is about the change that characterizes a person's life from beginning to end. Throughout the variety and movement of her life, the poet finds there a changeless one—the eternal God.

Whatever is good and perfect comes to us from God

Change is uncontrollable. No matter how carefully we arrange our lives, something will invade and alter them. My father worked at a rewarding job until he retired; everything was set for him and my mother. But leukemia invaded, and he died at age 63. This story is repeated with endless variety in everyone's life. What is there that does not change? Only the God of love. All we need do is maintain a heart of faith in the one who is the same yesterday, today, and forever.

Lord, abiding in your love,

I have nothing to fear.

How can I be dismayed when you are near?

Keep me, Father, close to your heart.

"I am the LORD,
    and I do not change."
    Malachi 3:6

O Perfect Love

Words: Dorothy F. Gurney

Music: Joseph Barnby

O per - fect love, all hu - man thought tran - scend - ing,

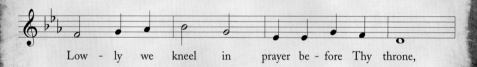

Low - ly we kneel in prayer be - fore Thy throne,

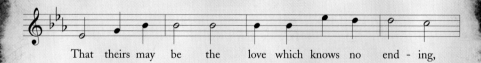

That theirs may be the love which knows no end - ing,

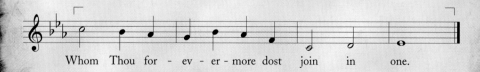

Whom Thou for - ev - er - more dost join in one.

O PERFECT LOVE,
ALL HUMAN THOUGHT
TRANSCENDING

O perfect Love, all human thought transcending,
Lowly we kneel in prayer before Thy throne,
That theirs may be the love which knows no ending,
Whom Thou forevermore dost join in one.

O perfect Life, be Thou their full assurance,
Of tender charity and steadfast faith,
Of patient hope and quiet, brave endurance,
With childlike trust that fears no pain nor death.

Grant them the joy which brightens earthly sorrow;
Grant them the peace which calms all earthly strife,
And to life's day the glorious unknown morrow
That dawns upon eternal love and life.

"No eye has seen,
no ear has heard,
and no mind has imagined
what God has prepared
for those who love him."

1 Corinthians 2:9

THE KISS *of the sun for pardon,*
The song of the birds for mirth,
One is nearer God's heart in a garden
Than anywhere else on earth.

Have you ever seen this rhyme posted in a garden? It is a single verse in the poem "God's Garden" from a book of poems entitled *A Little Book of Quiet,* by Dorothy Blomfield Gurney (1858–1932) of London, England. She is the author of the wedding hymn "O Perfect Love."

Gurney wrote the song at the request of her sister. "The year was

God,
who is both
love and life,
can deeply
infuse the
human soul.

1883," Gurney recalled. "It was Sunday evening and we were enjoying hymn singing. A song that we all particularly enjoyed was 'O Strength and Stay'. . .Someone remarked, 'What a pity the words of this beautiful song should be unsuitable for a wedding!' My sister turned to me and challenged, 'What is the use of a sister who composes poetry if she cannot write new words to a favorite tune? I would like to use the tune at my wedding.' I picked up a hymnbook and said, 'If no one will disturb me, I will go into the library and see what I can do.' Within fifteen minutes I was back with the group and reading the words I had jotted down. The writing of the words was no effort whatever after the initial idea came to me of the twofold aspect of perfect union, love and life. I feel that God helped me write this song."

The fresh-made hymn was sung at Mrs. Gurney's sister's wedding. After that it was used at weddings of British royalty and in many other fashionable London nuptials. In fact, the tune most used with these lyrics was composed by the prominent British organist, composer, and conductor Sir Joseph Barnby especially for the wedding of Princess Louise of Wales in 1889.

When Dorothy Gurney died, the *London Times* reported: "Thousands of people at thousands of weddings must have sung, or heard sung, 'O Perfect Love' without knowing that Mrs. Gurney wrote the hymn. It was always to her a matter of amused regret that she did not get a royalty for each performance. . . .

"But it is not as an author that she will be best remembered by her many friends. . . . A wide circle of friends of every creed and class knew that they could take to her all their troubles, great or small, and come away with the burden of them lightened or removed."

This hymn reveals a twofold love in the heart of Dorothy Gurney. She surely had these passions to be able to write this lyric prayer for a wedded couple. First, she loved her sister and cared very much about her approaching marriage. Gurney also loved God with such affection that she received a precious and true glimpse of the divine mystery—that God, who is both love and life, can deeply infuse the human soul. This perfect union is the goal of God's eternal purpose.

Heavenly Father, I pray a simple prayer,

which only you can answer—

that everyone would know the

love of Christ that surpasses knowledge,

so that they can be filled with

all the fullness of God.

Let us be glad and rejoice and honor him.
For the time has come for the wedding feast of the Lamb,
and his bride has prepared herself.
She is permitted to wear the finest white linen."

. . .And the angel said,

"Write this: Blessed are those who are invited
to the wedding feast of the Lamb."

And he added,

"These are true words that come from God."
Revelation 19:7–9

The King of Love My Shepherd Is

Words: Henry W. Baker

Music: John B. Dykes

The King of love my Shep - herd is, Whose

good - ness fail - eth nev - er; I noth - ing lack if

I am His And He is mine for - ev - er.

THE KING OF LOVE
MY SHEPHERD IS

The King of love my Shepherd is, Whose goodness faileth never,
I nothing lack if I am His and He is mine forever.

Where streams of living water flow my ransomed soul He leadeth,
And where the verdant pastures grow, with food celestial feedeth.

Perverse and foolish oft I strayed, but yet in love He sought me,
And on His shoulder gently laid, and home, rejoicing, brought me.

In death's dark vale I fear no ill with Thee, dear Lord, beside me;
Thy rod and staf my comfort still, Thy cross before to guide me.

Thou spread'st a table in my sight; Thy unction grace bestoweth;
And O what transport of delight from Thy pure chalice floweth!

The LORD is my shepherd;
I shall not want.
He makes me lie down in green pastures;
he leads me beside still waters;
he restores my soul.
He leads me in right paths for his name's sake.

Even though I walk through the darkest valley,
I fear no evil; for you are with me;
your rod and your staff–they comfort me.

You prepare a table before me in the presence of my enemies;
you anoint my head with oil;
my cup overflows.
Surely goodness and mercy shall follow me
all the days of my life,
and I shall dwell in the house of the LORD
my whole life long.

Psalm 23:1–6 NRSV

THERE was a hymnal called *Hymns Ancient and Modern* that sold sixty million copies in the late nineteenth century. That is not only historical, it is astonishing. One of its contributors (and its editor in chief from 1860 to 1877) was the aristocratic clergyman Henry Williams Baker, the author of "The King of Love My Shepherd Is"– the hymn that was sung at the funeral of Diana, Princess of Wales, in Westminster Abbey, London, on September 6, 1997.

As you can see from the lyrics given here, Baker's hymn is roughly based on the familiar Twenty-third Psalm. Let's think about the first line of the hymn: *The King of love my Shepherd is*. Without worrying about meter and rhyme, we can turn this sentence around to the way its thought would usually be expressed: "My shepherd is the king of love." This statement seems faulty because it mixes the images of king and shepherd. Kings are high. Shepherds are low. The shepherd herds sheep just as the cowboy herds cattle. Both tend livestock—a job you do if you can't get other kind of work. It is dirty and lonely and doesn't pay well. On this job you are the boss of nobody, only animals.

A king, though, is the boss of everybody. He is the direct opposite of a shepherd. Yet the song says "the king of love my shepherd is." How can one person simultaneously be the highest of all and the lowliest? A mystery, indeed. In fact, it is the mystery of God who became the man named Jesus Christ. Scholars believe that the very earliest Christians sang a hymn about this mystery. The words to this hymn are found in the New Testament. Here is a paraphrase of its beginning:

> *Though he was in the form of God,*
> *He did not suppose that his equality with God*
> *was something to take advantage of.*
> *Instead he emptied himself, taking the form of a slave,*
> *and was born in human likeness.*
> *And being found in human form,*
> *he humbled himself and became obedient*
> *to the point of death–even death on a cross.*

The verses, Philippians 2:6–8, express the same inexplicable mystery as Psalm 23:1. As the human mind approaches this mystery, its impulse is to worship the marvelous God of our Lord Jesus Christ; so the earliest of the believers bowed on their knees to sing this hymn.

Lord Jesus Christ, cause more people to bow in awe and prayer because of the truth and mystery of your incarnation. Thank you for your perfect human life, your death on that horrible cross, and for returning from death to bring life to all people who believe.

Because of this,
God raised him up to the heights of heaven
and gave him a name

that is above every other name,

so that at the name of Jesus every knee will bow,
in heaven and on earth and under the earth,

and every tongue will confess
that Jesus Christ is Lord,
to the glory of God the Father.

Philippians 2:9–11

O Sacred Head, Now Wounded

Words: Paul Gerhardt

Music: Hans Leo Hassler

Based on Latin poem ascribed to Bernard of Clairvaux

O sa-cred Head, now wound-ed, With grief and shame weighed down,

Now scorn-ful-ly sur-round-ed With thorns Thine on-ly crown:

How pale Thou art with an-guish, With sore a-buse and scorn,

How does that vis-age lan-guish, Which once was bright as morn!

O Sacred Head,
Now Wounded

O sacred Head, now wounded, with grief and shame weighed down,
Now scornfully surrounded with thorns, Thine only crown;
How pale Thou art with anguish, with sore abuse and scorn!
How does that visage languish, which once was bright as morn!

What Thou, my Lord, hast suffered, was all for sinners' gain;
Mine, mine was the transgression, but Thine the deadly pain.
Lo, here I fall, my Savior! 'Tis I deserve Thy place;
Look on me with Thy favor, vouchsafe to me Thy grace.

Men mock and taunt and jeer Thee, Thou noble countenance,
Though mighty worlds shall fear Thee and flee before Thy glance.
How art thou pale with anguish, with sore abuse and scorn!
How doth Thy visage languish that once was bright as morn!

Now from Thy cheeks has vanished their color once so fair;
From Thy red lips is banished the splendor that was there.
Grim death, with cruel rigor, hath robbed Thee of Thy life;
Thus Thou hast lost Thy vigor, Thy strength in this sad strife.

My burden in Thy Passion, Lord, Thou hast borne for me,
For it was my transgression which brought this woe on Thee.
I cast me down before Thee, wrath were my rightful lot;
Have mercy, I implore Thee; Redeemer, spurn me not!

What language shall I borrow to thank Thee, dearest friend,
For this Thy dying sorrow, Thy pity without end?
O make me Thine forever, and should I fainting be,
Lord, let me never, never outlive my love to Thee.

continued

65

My shepherd, now receive me; my guardian, own me Thine.
Great blessings Thou didst give me, O source of gifts divine.
Thy lips have often fed me with words of truth and love;
Thy Spirit oft hath led me to heavenly joys above.

Here I will stand beside Thee, from Thee I will not part;
O Savior, do not chide me! When breaks Thy loving heart,
When soul and body languish in death's cold, cruel grasp,
Then, in Thy deepest anguish, Thee in mine arms I'll clasp.

The joy can never be spoken, above all joys beside,
When in Thy body broken I thus with safety hide.
O Lord of Life, desiring Thy glory now to see,
Beside Thy cross expiring, I'd breathe my soul to Thee.

My Savior, be Thou near me when death is at my door;
Then let Thy presence cheer me, forsake me nevermore!
When soul and body languish, oh, leave me not alone,
But take away mine anguish by virtue of Thine own!

Be Thou my consolation, my shield when I must die;
Remind me of Thy passion when my last hour draws nigh.
Mine eyes shall then behold Thee, upon Thy cross shall dwell,
My heart by faith enfolds Thee. Who dieth thus dies well.

*It was our weaknesses he carried; it was our sorrows
that weighed him down. And we thought his troubles were
a punishment from God for his own sins!
But he was wounded and crushed for our sins.
He was beaten that we might have peace.
He was whipped, and we were healed!
All of us have strayed away like sheep.
We have left God's paths to follow our own.
Yet the LORD laid on him the guilt and sins of us all.*

Isaiah 53:4–6

A TENTH-CENTURY monk is credited with writing "O Sacred Head Now Wounded." Bernard of Clairvaux was active in the politics of the church as a diplomat and confidant of popes. He was also a prominent preacher and theologian. His devotion to and love of Christ is unquestioned. In fact, the reformer Martin Luther himself said, "Bernard loved Jesus as much as anyone can."

The words for this hymn are a part of a seven-section poem that considers the crucified Christ. Each section is a meditation on a different part of the Lord's body—a vision, a revelation of the suffering Christ as seen by one who loves him dearly. But Bernard of Clairvaux did not write his poem to be used as a hymn. In his day there was no hymn singing as we know it today.

Before the advent of Jesus Christ, professional singers sang psalms for worship in the Hebrew Temple, which is the basis of singing in Christian worship. The earliest fully preserved text of a Christian hymn is a poem written in Greek in about A.D. 200 or earlier. We know it as "Go, Gladsome Light," translated by the nineteenth-century American poet Henry Wadsworth Longfellow.

Hymns began to develop after the Roman emperor Constantine legalized Christianity in A.D. 313. Hilary of Poitiers composed a book of hymn texts in about A.D. 360 and soon Ambrose of Milan brought congregational singing into the church. These early hymns were sung to simple, possibly folk, melodies. Their lyrics were drawn from Christian Latin poetry of the period.

Here I will stand beside Thee, from Thee I will not part.

By the time of Bernard of Clairvaux, trained choirs had replaced the congregation in the singing of hymns. New, more ornate melodies were composed and many earlier melodies were embellished. Congregational singing was reestablished by Martin Luther (1483–1546) and the Protestant Reformation, mainly in the German Lutheran Church. Early German hymn melodies were unharmonized and sung unaccompanied, although combinations of choir, organ, and harmony appeared later. The earliest Protestant hymn collection was that of Luther and Johann Walther, published in 1524.

The father of the English hymn is Isaac Watts (1674–1748). He lamented the condition of music in the church of his day. "The singing of God's praise is the part of worship most closely related to heaven; but its performance among us is the worst on earth." Today, churches are abandoning the great hymns of the past; the hymns of Bernard, Watts, Wesley, Crosby, and hundreds of other hymnists. I believe this is a great loss to believers everywhere. Although modern praise choruses have their place, may they never replace the church's rich treasury of hymns.

Where can I find the words to thank you, my dearest friend, for your sorrow in dying, and for your endless mercy upon the human race? Make me yours forever, and if I become weak, Lord Jesus, let me never, never outlive my love for you.

They made a crown
of long, sharp thorns
and put it on his head,

and they placed a stick
in his right hand as a scepter.

Then they knelt before him in mockery, yelling,
"Hail! King of the Jews!"

And they spit on him
and grabbed the stick and beat him
on the head with it.

Matthew 27:29–30

The Head That Once Was Crowned with Thorns

Words: Thomas Kelly

Music: Jeremiah Clarke

The Head that once was crowned with thorns Is

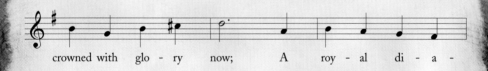

crowned with glo - ry now; A roy - al di - a -

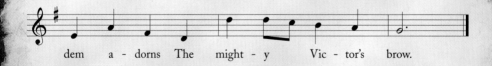

dem a - dorns The might - y Vic - tor's brow.

THE HEAD THAT ONCE
WAS CROWNED WITH THORNS

The head that once was crowned with thorns
Is crowned with glory now;
A royal diadem adorns
The mighty victor's brow.

The highest place that heaven affords
Belongs to Him by right;
The King of kings and Lord of lords,
And heaven's eternal Light.

The joy of all who dwell above,
The joy of all below,
To whom He manifests His love,
And grants His Name to know.

What we do see is Jesus, who
"for a little while was made lower
than the angels"

and now is "crowned with glory and honor"
because he suffered death for us.

Yes, by God's grace,

Jesus tasted death
for everyone in all the world.
Hebrews 2:9

WHAT would Jesus do? This question was present everywhere in Christianity a few years ago. All kinds of Christians were asking themselves this question; some still are. It is meant to be a guide to right living. Personally, I don't ask myself that question. I find it frightening.

What would Jesus do? The Four Gospels furnish the answer: He would die a lonely, miserable, brutal death—a victorious death that achieved redemption for the entire creation. I don't ask that question because the gospel has been answering it for two millennia. What would Jesus do in this or that situation? He would die.

The apostle Paul's letters tell a lot about right living. Here is what he wrote to the people living in the ancient city of Philippi, now located in Greece: "Don't be selfish; don't live to make a good impression on others. Be humble, thinking of others as better than yourself. Don't think only about your own affairs, but be interested in others, too, and what they are doing. Your attitude should be the same that Christ Jesus had" (Philippians 2:3–5).

The next five verses describe the attitude of Christ Jesus. "Though he was God," Paul writes, "he did not demand and cling to his rights as God" (Philippians 2:6). Instead, he made himself nothing, took the humble position of a slave, and appeared in human form. Finally, he "obediently humbled himself further by dying a criminal's death on a cross" (vv. 7–8).

That is what Jesus did. His life is God's love for the world.

Christians should ask themselves a different question—What should I do? What is my attitude toward God's love in Christ? The hymn "The Head That Once Was Crowned with Thorns" says, "To whom he manifests his love, and grants his name to know, to them the cross with all its shame, with all its grace, is given."

Paul saw God's love. He knew the name that is above every name. And though he was an accomplished man with a high position in the Jewish world, he said, "I consider them worthless because of what Christ has done. Yes, everything else is worthless when compared with the priceless gain of knowing Christ Jesus my Lord" (Philippians 3:7–8).

The Apostle continues: "I have discarded everything else, counting it all as garbage, so that I may have Christ and become one with him" (vv. 8–9). This shows that Paul's attitude was the same as Christ's. The hymn describes it like this: "They suffer with their Lord below; they reign with Him above."

Inevitably, though, a question rises in everyone's heart, mine included. The question contradicts Christ's temperament, but no matter how you try to keep it down, the question still pops up—*What's in it for me?* The hymn's soaring answer is in harmony with the glorious gospel of God: "Their profit and their joy is to know the mystery of His love."

Dearest God, thank you for your Son, Jesus
Christ. Thank you that he was obedient to
your eternal plan and died on a cross.
And thank you that you have given me
the grace to bow down on my knees
and confess that Jesus Christ is Lord.

God showed how much he loved us
by sending his only Son
into the world
so that we might have eternal life through him.

This is real love.
It is not that we loved God,
but that he loved us and sent his Son
as a sacrifice to take away our sins.
1 John 4:9–10

When I Survey the Wondrous Cross

Words: Isaac Watts

Music: Edward Miller

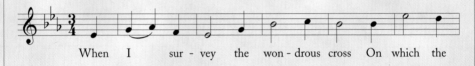

When I sur - vey the won - drous cross On which the

Prince of Glo - ry died, My rich - est gain I

count but loss And pour con - tempt on all my pride.

WHEN I SURVEY
THE WONDROUS CROSS

When I survey the wondrous cross
On which the Prince of glory died,
My richest gain I count but loss,
And pour contempt on all my pride.

Forbid it, Lord, that I should boast,
Save in the death of Christ my God!
All the vain things that charm me most,
I sacrifice them to His blood.

See from His head, His hands, His feet,
Sorrow and love flow mingled down!
Did e'er such love and sorrow meet,
Or thorns compose so rich a crown?

As for me, God forbid
that I should boast about anything
except the cross of our Lord Jesus Christ.

Because of that cross,

my interest in this world died long ago,
and the world's interest in me is also long dead.

Galatians 6:14

IT IS an understatement to say that Isaac Watts was a precocious child. He learned Latin at age five, Greek at nine, French at eleven, and when he was twelve he mastered Hebrew. His habit of spontaneously making rhymes as he spoke drove his father to distraction. Watts grew up to be an Nonconformist cleric and eventually wrote over six hundred hymns. Today he is known as the father of English hymnody.

Watts wrote "When I Survey the Wondrous Cross" when he was thirty-four years old. British poet Matthew Arnold (1822–1888) called it the greatest hymn in the English language. This is high praise coming as it does from the preeminent literary critic of the nineteenth century who occupied the chair of poetry at Oxford University.

The hymn's powerful images and strong emotion combine with its author's pure devotion to God. The blend is a strengthening tonic for a believer's faith. Watts wrote the hymn as he was preparing to take Communion, an event central to the Christian faith because it memorializes Christ's work of redemption through his death on the cross—the single most significant act in human history.

Isaac Watts presided over the service of the Lord's Table as pastor of Mark Lane Independent (i.e., Congregational) Chapel, London, from 1699 until his health declined in 1712. Here Watts wrote and published most of his hymns. As he served the Eucharist, the young minister may have said words similar to these:

On the night he was handed over to suffering and death, our Lord Jesus Christ took bread; and when he had given thanks, he broke it, and gave it to his disciples, and said, "Take, eat: This is my body which is given for you. Do this for the remembrance of me."

After supper he took the cup of wine; and when he had given thanks, he gave it to them, and said, "Drink this, all of you: This is my blood of

the new covenant, which is shed for you and for many for the forgiveness
of sins. Whenever you drink it, do this for the remembrance of me."

Therefore we proclaim the mystery of faith: Christ has died. Christ is
*risen. Christ will come again.**

The second verse of this moving hymn expresses the centrality of
the death of Jesus Christ in a believer's life:

> *Forbid it, Lord, that I should boast,*
> *Save in the death of Christ my God!*
> *All the vain things that charm me most,*
> *I sacrifice them to His blood.*

The Communion service is a reminder of the vast importance of
Christ's death. Isaac Watts said that Christ's death expresses "Love so
amazing, so divine." It is really beyond words. Yet the words of
Watts's hymn "When I Survey the Wondrous Cross" are his superb
attempt to express the immense mystery of Christ's crucifixion.

* *The Book of Common Prayer.* New York: The Church Hymnal Corporation, 1979.
  pp. 362–63.

Lord, when my heart sees the wondrous cross on which you died, I have to count everything I have as loss and pour contempt on all my pride. Lord, don't let me boast about anything except your death. I sacrifice all the vain things that charm me most to your blood.

*Carrying the cross
by himself,*

*Jesus went to the place called Skull Hill
(in Hebrew, Golgotha).*

*There they
crucified him.*

John 19:18–19

O Love That Wilt Not Let Me Go

Words: George Matheson

Music: Albert L. Peace

O Love that wilt not let me go, I rest my wea-ry soul in

Thee; I give Thee back the life I owe, That

in Thine o-cean depths its flow May rich – er, full – er be.

O LOVE THAT WILT
NOT LET ME GO

O Love that wilt not let me go,
I rest my weary soul in thee;
I give thee back the life I owe,
That in thine ocean depths its flow
May richer, fuller be.

O Light that followest all my way,
I yield my flickering torch to thee;
My heart restores its borrowed ray,
That in thy sunshine's blaze its day
May brighter, fairer be.

O Joy that seekest me through pain,
I cannot close my heart to thee;
I trace the rainbow through the rain,
And feel the promise is not vain,
That morn shall tearless be.

See how very much
our heavenly Father
loves us,

for he allows us to be called
his children,
and we really are!
1 John 3:1

GEORGE Matheson (1842–1906) was born with poor eyesight, which gradually worsened until he was nearly blind. But he was academically gifted and so studied for the ministry with the help of his sisters. As pastor for the Church of Scotland in the resort town of Innelan, Matheson would memorize sermons and recite the Scriptures verbatim. When he preached, some listeners were unaware of his handicap.

I trace the rainbow through the rain, and feel the promise is not vain, that morn shall tearless be.

He wrote this hymn in the parsonage (manse) at Innelan in June 1882. "I was forty years of age," Matheson recalled. "I was alone in the manse at that time. It was the night of my sister's marriage, and the rest of the family were staying overnight in Glasgow. Something happened to me, which was known only to myself, and which caused me the most severe mental suffering. The hymn was the fruit of that suffering."

What was Matheson's suffering? He never said. But others guessed it was rejection by his fiancée. Apparently she didn't know her future husband's destiny included blindness until shortly before their wedding. It is said she then informed Matheson, "I do not wish to be the wife of a blind preacher." That's called brutal honesty.

Concerning his hymn, Matheson said,

It was the quickest bit of work I ever did in my life. I had the impression of having it dictated to me by some inward voice rather than of working it out myself. I am quite sure that the whole work was completed in five minutes, and equally sure that it never received at my hands any retouching or correction. I have no natural gift of rhythm. All the other verses I have ever written are manufactured articles; this came like a dayspring from on high.

Reread the hymn and see what George Matheson made of the disappointment of a lifetime. The apostle Paul also had a severe suffering. He called it a *thorn in the flesh.* "Three different times I begged the Lord to take it away," Paul said in 2 Corinthians 12:8. But instead of taking the suffering away, the Lord gave Paul something more:

Each time he said, "My gracious favor is all you need. My power works best in your weakness." So now I am glad to boast about my weaknesses, so that the power of Christ may work through me (2 Corinthians 12:9).

George Matheson, it seems, found the secret of living with suffering. He took God's grace, and his weakness was changed into the power of Christ. Paul did the same and received the divine power to establish the truth of the gospel for all time. In the same power, the power that is perfected in human weakness, Matheson wrote this most encouraging hymn.

Since I know it is all for Christ's good,
I am quite content with my weaknesses
and with insults, hardships, persecutions,
and calamities.

For when I am weak,
then I am strong.
2 Corinthians 12:10

But the Lord said,

"...[Paul] is my chosen instrument
to take my message
to the Gentiles
and to kings,
as well as to the people of Israel.

And I will show him
how much he must suffer
for me."

Acts 9:15–16

THIS book is one in a series of four collections of hymn meditations by Daniel Partner, a writer and musician. His other recent books include *A Cloud of Witnesses—Fifty Readings on Women of Faith* (Fleming H. Revell, 2000) which he co-authored with his wife Margaret, and *The Story of Jesus—A Portrait of Christ from the Gospels* (Barbour, 2000). Daniel lives with his family in Sisters, Oregon.

HYMNS OF GOD'S LOVE
CD TRACK LISTING

1   O the Deep, Deep Love of Jesus–Harp & Strings (3:41)

2   Amazing Grace–Celtic Sounds (3:28)

3   Love Divine, All Loves Excelling–Flute & Guitar (3:08)

4   Jesus, Lover of My Soul–Cello (2:12)

5   Jesus Thy Blood and Righteousness–Classical Piano (2:23)

6   In Heavenly Love Abiding–Saxophone (3:05)

7   O Perfect Love–Cello (3:31)

8   The King of Love My Shepherd Is–Celtic Sounds (2:46)

9   O Sacred Head Now Wounded–Classical Piano (3:26)

10   The Head That Once Was Crowned with Thorns–
      Saxophone (2:23)

11   When I Survey the Wondrous Cross–Celtic Sounds (2:48)

12   O Love That Wilt Not Let Me Go–Cello (2:44)